PEACOCK NEW NAME

(American Traditional) retold by Cynthia Rider

Illustrated by Louise Ellis

One day, a peacock came to Meadow Farm. All the animals ran to look at him. Peacock smiled at them. He put his head on one side and said, "Look at this!"

Peacock spread his tail feathers into a shining fan.

"Oh my!" said Hen.

"He's beautiful!" said Cat.

"Steady on," said Dog. "That bird is a big-head already. Don't make him worse."

When the farmer came along, he gave Peacock some bread.

"Here you are, Peaky-Pops," he said. "Eat your breakfast and enjoy the sunny weather."

"Peaky-Pops!" said Peacock. "What a dreadful name!"

"It's all right," said Hen. "He gives us all pet names. He calls me Chick. Cat's name is Kitty, and Dog is Sam."

Peacock put his head in the air.

"But I am very grand," he said, "and I need a very grand name. So my new name will be: Beautiful-is-the-bird-with-the-feathers-that-shine-like-treasure.

If you call me anything else," he said, "I shall peck you to death."

"How dreadful!" squawked Hen. "Please don't do that, Beautiful-is-the-bird-with-the-feathers-that-shine-like-treasure."

Hen and Peacock ate their breakfast. They didn't see the stealthy fox who was treading softly across the meadow.

"That bird with the long feathers looks tasty," said the fox. Then he leapt over the wall and grabbed Peacock.

"Help, Hen!" yelled Peacock.
"Tell Cat to save me."
Hen got ready to run.

"I'll tell her at once, Beautiful-is-the-bird-with-the-feathers-that-shine-like-treasure," she said.

"Cat, Cat, the fox has got Beautiful-is-the-bird-with-the-feathers-that-shine-like-treasure," shouted Hen.

"Got WHO?" said Cat.

"It's Peacock's new name," said Hen. "He says we've got to use it or he'll peck us to death."

"How dreadful!" said Cat. But she wanted to help Peacock, so she ran to tell Dog.

"I must tell my Master," said Dog, and he leapt away.

"Don't forget to use Peacock's new name," shouted Cat, "or he'll peck you to death."

Dog ran till he was out of breath.

"Master, Master, the fox has got Beautiful-is-the-bird-with-the-feathers-that-shine-like-treasure," he panted. "He's taken him across the meadow already, and now he's heading for his den."

The farmer shook his head. "I don't know anyone with a silly name like that," he said.

"Yes, you do," said Dog. "It's Peacock's new name, and if you don't call him by it, he says he'll peck you to death."

"I'll give him *peck me to death!*" shouted the farmer. He took his heavy stick and set off across the meadow . . .

and he got to the fox's den just in time!

"If the fox ever gets me again," said Peacock, "just call me Peaky-Pops."

"We will," said Hen.

"We will," said Cat.

"We will, Peaky-Pops," said Dog.